MaY(be a) sign(post) to paradise?(!)

Joachim Kranzen

MaY(be a) sign(post) to paradise?(!)

Joachim Kranzen

Imprint

Bibliografische Information der Deutschen Nationalbibliothek: Die Deutsche Nationalbibliothek verzeichnet diese Publikation in der Deutschen Nationalbibliografie; detaillierte bibliografische Daten sind im Internet über http://dnb.dnb.de abrufbar.

© 2023 Joachim Kranzen

Herstellung und Verlag: BoD – Books on Demand, Norderstedt

ISBN: 978-3-7578-2552-2

table of content

preface 13

Isaiah 38: healing...14

Ephesians 2: live..15

Genesis 2: Eden 16

Luke 12: warnings..17

Deuteronomy 5: ten 18

Romans 15: responsibility 19

Ruth 2: attention..20

Colossians 2: strength..21

Deuteronomy 23: purification.................................22

2. Thessalonians 2: blinding 23

Jeremiah 31: eternity..24

Matthew 5: different 25

Isaiah 31: size...26

1. Thimothy 1: truthfulness 27

Psalms 25: grace 28

Luke 15: find back..29

Numbers 14: trust in God.......................................30

Luke 1: announcement 31

Psalms 34: rest 32

Philippians 4: grattitude 33

Judges 1: good 36

1. Thessalonians 1: strive 37

Joshua 22: beware 38

Hebrews 10: caution 39

Psalms 50: fear 40

Luke 17: worship of God 41

Psalms 89: immutability 42

Kolossians 1: solidarity 43

Jeremiah 17: sabbath 44

Revelation 21: glory 45

Psalms 102: endure 46

Romans 15: peace 47

Psalms 25: trust 48

John 15: confidence 49

Isaiah 64: rebuilding 50

Galatians 3: freedom 51

Ezekiel 46: serve 52

1. Corinthians 1: equality 53

Job 16: overview 54

Acts 4: frankness 55

Jona 4: anger...56

Luke 19: trade..57

about myself...58

for the Glory and Honor of God

PREFACE

It was in the summer of 2023 when I once again consciously took time for God. The question that came to me in a church service at the beginning of May and which formed the basis for a three-week holiday was: "Am I already living in paradise?"

At the beginning of June it was time. Mainly I wanted to concentrate on God's word and not let myself be unnecessarily distracted by e-mails, calls, etc., so I turned off my smartphone as much as possible. Morning and evening I read his word, the bible, and just let him guide me.

Accompany me a part of the way that God has shown me and maybe you will find a signpost for your way to paradise. Anyway, I wish you the best.

I read one chapter each day from the Old Testament and one from the New Testament and wrote out the verse that spoke to me the most. In order to really understand the content of this book, you cannot avoid reading the Bible.

God's blessings to you now and a beautiful and fulfilling way back to paradise.

Monday, June, 5th, 2023

ISAIAH 38: HEALING

Here someone is terminally ill and receives the message that he is going to die soon. Thereupon he turns to God with supplications and requests and he gives him a few more years of life as a gift.

verse 15

How heavenly does something like that feel?

If at all, do you only turn to God in "difficult situations" or also with everyday little things?

Have you ever thought about asking God to open your eyes to His paradise?

EPHESIANS 2: LIVE

With the resurrection in the Christian faith, our previous sins are forgiven because God is merciful. He is our peace and in Christ we are all one, regardless of our earthly origin. This forgiveness is the most important step in order to even get a view of paradise again. verse 19

Have you ever thought about how it looks to you?

Tuesday, June, 6th, 2023

GENESIS 2: EDEN

God created everything and gives life. He gives us food and drink out of His bounty, and He also created the tree of the knowledge of good and evil to show us boundaries we must not cross. verse 8

Is there someone near to you who does everything to ensure that you exceed these limits?

When that happens, do you turn back to God and ask His forgiveness?

LUKE 12: WARNINGS

God sets boundaries and warns us not to backbite or worry about anything. It also does us good to be wary of the leaven of false preachers and to be ever vigilant. In addition, it strengthens our innermost being when we stand before the world to God and thus to our Christian faith, without fear of anything. Jesus already says there will be people who will then turn away from us; they are welcome to do. verse 29

Are you worried?

Are you always alert?

Wednesday, June, 7th, 2023

A day of gardening and starting to write this book.

DEUTERONOMY 5: TEN

With the 10 commandments, God gave us everything we need to live in paradise. Even here and now. verse 24

How do you feel about that?

ROMANS 15: RESPONSIBILITY

What if we took more responsibility for our brothers and sisters (both physical and spiritual)?

When the strong take on the weaknesses of the weak and support them?

If we were more unanimous and perhaps showed more hospitality to one another?

Is Jesus Christ the only true reason you are building on?

Do you share your spiritual goods that God gives you with others?

verse 13

Thursday, June, 8th, 2023

RUTH 2: ATTENTION

If we do not leave God's field, he will fill and exalt us. verse 8

Have you ever thought about plowing the field of God in your personal environment from time to time without wanting to "proselytize"?

Do you share the Bible with others?

Do you also value little and take care of it?

Are you selfish?

Those who follow God stand out. Ever thought about it?

COLOSSIANS 2: STRENGTH

In Christ all the treasures of wisdom and knowledge are hidden. Gratitude helps us recognize this and see our way.

Did you know, right?

At the same time, it is good to be wary of people's philosophy and empty deceit. Statements regarding faith can always be checked against the Bible, so as not to be taken in by false doctrine.

Is that what you do?

Luckily Jesus Christ canceled our promissory note and there is no one who can put a promissory note on us again. He alone is the lord over all powers and authorities.

Any questitions?

verse 2

Friday, June, 9th, 2023

DEUTERONOMY 23: PURIFICATION

God only accepts what is pure. God helps us to keep our spiritual bodies clean as best we can. If we don't let that dissuade us, we'll get a clearer view again. verse 26

Did you know that?

2. THESSALONIANS 2: BLINDING

Satan tries to turn people away from believing in Jesus Christ. In many people we see that lawlessness toward God is already at work and is increasing. God blinds those who are perishing to believe the heresies of Satan. verse 13

Do you notice things like that too?

How do you feel about it yourself?

Do you check from time to time whether you've been caught in another heresy?

Saturday, June, 10th, 2023

JEREMIAH 31: ETERNITY

God helps us to eliminate what does not correspond to Him in us. Thereby he enables us to see and reach the paradise in us and around us again. When you turn to God, real joy will enter your heart again. verse 33

Is there joy or sadness in your heart?

MATTHEW 5: DIFFERENT

Blessed are those who do not conform to what the world dictates and do not hide themselves, but step forward and are a light to those who sit in darkness. verse 20

Do you too often focus on worldly things?

How about you with personal action in all areas?

Did you know that God rewards such things?

And of course you always knew that Christians don't take oaths?

Sunday, June, 11th, 2023

ISAIAH 31: SIZE

Anyone who relies on the supposed strength of people will fail. If God will fight, nothing can stand against it. verse 1

Who do you think is ultimately stronger?

1. THIMOTHY 1: TRUTHFULNESS

Holding on to love with a pure heart and unfeigned faith, as we have learned about Jesus, will sooner or later bring us rich rewards. Maybe not according to what people understand by reward, but that needn't concern us. verse 5

How is your love for the people around you?

And towards people you don't know?

Monday, June, 12th, 2023

PSALMS 25: GRACE

Those who faithfully follow God, stick to Him and do not follow human fables, they will know and possess Paradise. But whoever acts unfaithfully will be held accountable. But to those who keep the covenant and testimonies of Christ, God is faithful and gracious.

verse 9

Have you ever experienced this faithfulness and grace of God?

Do you really not follow human fables?

LUKE 15: FIND BACK

God rejoices in every sinner who sincerely repents. Whoever turns to God with a sincere heart (he knows if it is sincere!) and turns away from evil, he accepts. A reversal is possible at any time and from any situation. Anyone who is with God can draw from the full and does not have to wait for a specific point in time. verse 31

Are you easily persuaded to lie like "God won't take you out of the situation (anymore)!" or "You can't (so easily) get out of it now!"?

Do you sometimes tell yourself that nonsense?

Tuesday, June, 13th, 2023

NUMBERS 14: TRUST IN GOD

God wants us to trust him even in difficult situations, the outcome of which we cannot see. Who trusts God, with him is God! verse 45

How does it feel when you experience something like this?

Of course you already found out, didn't you?

LUKE 1: ANNOUNCEMENT

God announces great events and whoever believes in him will experience great salvation, because God helps those who trust in him, even if it sometimes takes a little longer. Those who are not afraid of men can serve God without fear and be a light to others, always setting their feet on the path of peace. Verses 46+47

Have you ever experienced this help from God?

How did it feel?

Wednesday, June, 14th, 2023

PSALMS 34: REST

Keep your eyes and mind always on God and fear only God and no one else. Whoever does this enters the rest of God in order to be prepared for something new. verse 2

Have you always fixed your eyes and mind on God?

What, or rather who, are you afraid of?

Have you ever been in the rest of God?

If not, why not?

PHILIPPIANS 4: GRATTITUDE

This is about always seeking unity with one another and not worrying about anything. When we learn about lack or abundance, it is only to empathize with those who have either and cannot cope. verse 13

Are you always looking for unity?

Is there anything that separates or wants to separate you from others and that you are therefore afraid of?

the scent of the *wind*

(originated in the Eselsburg valley lying under a tree)

You are lying on a mild summer day

with closed eyes in the grass

The wind blows sometimes stronger and sometimes very weakly

The grasses occasionally caress your feet and your face

You smell the grass, the approaching summer

The leaves of the tree in whose shade you lie rustle

Sometimes louder, sometimes quieter

You feel the wind as it blows across your face

and strokes your whole body

Your thoughts literally fly away with the wind

Now and then you hear the croaking of the frogs,

who have gathered by the river

You sit down and feel the gusts of wind

Like the grass around you

you let them rock you back and forth

Not because the wind is so strong

but because of the lightness in you

The grass shows waves like the water in the sea

In between, the crickets are chirping

Like the grass, you have a firm anchor in the here and now

and still experience the lightness of being

Thursday, June, 15th, 2023

JUDGES 1: GOOD

God has already prepared the way to paradise for us. It is up to us to start. Supporting one another and following God's instructions closely will help us to be successful. And it's always good, before we do anything, to ask God about it first. verse 2

By the time you read this book you've already started. But did you go off consciously or unconsciously?

1. THESSALONIANS 1: STRIVE

In order to get to paradise, it takes not only God's Word, but also the Holy Spirit. We can ask God for this in prayer. Our goal is not to be like Jesus, but the people around us can see that we are building on God and on nothing else.

verse 8

Do you worship God or do you worship other things?

Do you feel uncomfortable when those around you see that you have God as your foundation (when you already have)?

Friday, June, 16th, 2023

JOSHUA 22: BEWARE

When it comes to larger matters, it is good to always "sleep over it" and talk to each other to understand what the other person means. verse 5

Do you take the time to think things through thoroughly?

If we're being pressured to "sign immediately," then something is wrong and the damage will be greater than you think. Especially when it's "tempting"!

Come to rest!

HEBREWS 10: CAUTION

Did you know that with the death of Jesus the sacrifices stopped?

If you are already walking the path of God yourself, are you encouraging others who are also doing or planning to do so?

Especially when the going gets tough?

Do you stay away from sin and those who want to tempt you into it and turn you away from God's path?

Satan is always trying to take you away from paradise. Already clear, right?

Verses 35+36

Saturday, June, 17th, 2023

PSALMS 50: FEAR

We need only fear God, who can destroy more than the body, and nothing else. Whoever turns to God will be saved by Him. The worst thing that can happen to the wicked is that we are not afraid of them because we have inner strength through God. verse 23

Did you know that God can destroy more than just your body?

Likewise, that all who turn to him will be saved?

Are you aware of your inner strength or do you only look at your weaknesses and are afraid?

LUKE 17: WORSHIP OF GOD

Since only belief in God and nothing else gives us access to Paradise, it is good to trust God and to believe His Word alone. Faith and trust in God saves us. Therefore, there is no point in following human fables. Serving God truly sets us free. Then we will see that paradise is already within us and around us.

verse 19

Do you only believe in God or do you have (a few) other "gods"?

Have you ever used the Bible to check whether what other people tell you about faith is really true? (not an easy task, I know)

Have you ever experienced the freedom that God gives us?

If not, then I wish you the best.

If yes, how did it feel?

Sunday, June, 18th, 2023:

PSALMS 89: IMMUTABILITY

God forgives our iniquities when we turn to him. For what God has said remains so for all eternity. However, people who are against God twist His Word to turn others away from it. verse 35

Does your heart always have the attitude of wanting to hear God speak and fearing God?

Have you ever experienced that God is then just and faithful to you?

KOLOSSIANS 1: SOLIDARITY

If we are in prayer and thus in direct connection with God and always trust in the power and strength of the gospel, then God's power can have an effect in us. In addition, we can stand up for the brothers and sisters before God and include them in prayer. They too can claim the blood that Jesus shed on the cross at any time. verse 13

Have you ever experienced the stillness of prayer even when everything around you is noisy?

Have you ever experienced the inner lightness when you turn to God?

The calm and the strength that he gives you then?

A prayer doesn't have to be elaborate. This can also be a very simple "Thank you God".

If you've never done it before, don't just say, "Thank God," but try to say it consciously. Can you feel the difference?

Monday, June, 19th, 2023

JEREMIAH 17: SABBATH

He who turns away from idolatry, following only God and keeping the Lord's day holy, is like a tree planted by streams of water. verse 10

If you are totally broken, have you ever consciously taken time for God?

Or are you afraid of knowing how much more power this gives you than any stimulant?

REVELATION 21: GLORY

The chapter is again about the fact that everything impure remains outside of paradise and that it is not possible to describe the glory of paradise with human words. Neither calamity nor disease has an existence there. verse 25

How does it feel to think that there is no sickness or evil in paradise?

Are you one of those people who just have this stupid "we can't achieve that anyway" attitude all the time?

Is your gaze mainly focused on the "bad" around us?

Tuesday, June, 20th, 2023

PSALMS 102: ENDURE

God tests us with various afflictions. He discards and builds up when we stay close to God, even when things are "bad." For God is the same for all time. verse 2

You do realize that not everything is rosy with believing Christians?

That we too are not spared from illnesses and (financial) challenges?

But is it also clear to you that all of this serves to advance us in the spirit of God?

That we can always turn our gaze to God in order to gain strength and endurance, especially in difficult situations, which people who know nothing about God / don't want to know anything will never experience?

That we don't have to go through everything by ourselves?

And that everything is "only half as bad" (if at all still as much) because we trust in God, even when hard times hit us?

I can only confirm it from my own experience!

ROMANS 15: PEACE

Charity is one of the most important qualities. But note that you cannot give anything if you have nothing because you have burned out with charity: love your neighbor as YOURSELF! If we stick to it, then we always seek unity, not separation, and we take care that nobody self-destructs out of sheer charity. Then we will also carry within us a constant praise to God for everything we receive from him (even the trials he puts on us!), and a view of the path that God has designed for us, even if it is sometimes takes a little longer than we would like. verse 2

Have you ever thought about this?

Do you know people who have burned out out of sheer charity or who are threatened with it?

Do you always have praise for God, even if something doesn't go according to your ideas?

Wednesday, June, 21st, 2023

PSALMS 25: TRUST

It says here that whoever trusts in God will not be put to shame. For this, however, it is important to let God guide you on his way again and again and to seek God with a sincere heart. In addition, those who think not only of themselves, but also of others and stand up for the kingdom of God, have found the true treasure in heaven. verse 14

Do you have this treasure?

JOHN 15: CONFIDENCE

Those who stay close to God will see with different eyes and hear with different ears. We are equipped with a new sense to better understand God's words and actions. verse 15

How about having that sense?

Or to hear God speaking (again)?

ISAIAH 64: REBUILDING

God knows when to demolish and when to build. Even when everything around us is in ruins, it helps us if we hold steadfastly to God and ask him to rebuild. Whoever asks him for help and comes before him with supplication, thanksgiving and a pure heart, he will help at the right time. And if we keep an eye not only on ourselves but also on his realm, the reward will be all the greater. verse 11

Have you ever experienced what it means when God tears down and builds up again?

GALATIANS 3: FREEDOM

Those who live by faith in Jesus are free. The law is for the foolish. Those who follow Christ and align themselves with him no longer need the law. For Christ will guide us and put his mind on our minds and write on our hearts. verse 11

How do you feel when you imagine that all people have this purpose?

Friday, June, 23rd, 2023

EZEKIEL 46: SERVE

Everything is well arranged in the house of God, including mutual give and take. If you have something, you can also give it. However, no one should cause another to become poor as a result. Whoever follows God will know when, where, how and with whom he will share his (spiritual) possessions. verse 18

Do you know that feeling or do you always let yourself be persuaded by other people?

1. CORINTHIANS 1: EQUALITY

God humbles the high and exalts the low so that we may see His wisdom and greatness. He shows us that there is no reason for us to consider one person to be better than another. All are equal before God. verse 31

What do you think?

Saturday, June, 24th, 2023

JOB 16: OVERVIEW

Advice can sometimes seem like a beating, pity like scorn and mockery. You feel like the whole world and even God himself are against you. Then it is important to look towards paradise and life after death. But we can learn to see beyond what is around us.

verse 22

Do you know that?

ACTS 4: FRANKNESS

Those who walk with Jesus need not fear anything and can proclaim the gospel boldly. If you are questioned, God will give you the right words at the right time. Speak with boldness and witness to Jesus wherever you go, for He is the ruler of all powers and authorities. verse 13

When you speak about God, is it outspoken or always with a raised hand?

Have you ever had an "intuition" about what to say in a certain situation?

Sunday, June, 25th, 2023

JONA 4: ANGER

Here someone is angry with God because God does not do what the person thinks he will do.

Do you sometimes get angry when God calls you for a task and it doesn't go your way?

The road to paradise is definitely not going the way you imagine. But do you want to block your way with anger and always stand in your own way?

If then a "hot wind" comes and "the sun stings you", do you think you now have a right to anger?

Do you really want to go against the grace of God towards others?

God takes care of us so we don't have to worry.

Is it really that hard to turn to God and take shelter in his shadow?

Don't be frightened and don't be afraid of it when you then find peace for your unsettled soul and get a clear view of paradise again.

LUKE 19: TRADE

Those who act righteously, God will come and bless them. We have all been given a talent and can learn to use it properly and increase it by sharing it. verse 3

When you find your way back to paradise, do you share it with others?

Would you dare to share your experiences with God with others?

What could possibly come of it if you do?

ABOUT MYSELF

Hello, my Name ist Joachim Kranzen and I am glad that you are reading this book.

I'm not a priest, pastor or anything like that, but I've been walking with God for many years.

Professionally, I deal with coaching and have been self-employed since the beginning of 2010.

In my work as a coach, the Word of God forms the basis of how I work. Here and there I also point to verses from the Bible.

The coaching is about personal development, both in the private sphere and in everyday business life. In the private sphere, I show how you can find a way back to more contentment and serenity in the here and now.

In business corporate coaching, my focus is on team and corporate leadership. This is specifically about how to (further) develop teams and lead people without having to constantly give them instructions. How to motivate, get others out of their "hole" and the like.

CONCLUSION

If someone wants to "make things clear" to you using a verse from the Bible, then don't just leave this single verse, but the 7 before and the 7 after or the entire associated chapter. If you have the opportunity, then also compare different printed versions of the Bible. Then you get a clearer picture of what your counterpart is telling you and whether it is true.

For me there is no question that God exists and that he guides my life. That's why I entrusted my life to him alone a long time ago and set out on his path. God always shows me where he wants me and I can only encourage you to walk the path with God. It's not always easy, nor are we spared God's trials. But it is far more fulfilling than anything the world has to offer.

When I asked the question about paradise, I hadn't thought that a book would come out of it. When you have learned to ask the right questions, God will also give you something that no money in the world can weigh: you will feel when God wants something from you, what it will be and how you can share it with others . This gives you inner strength, calm and serenity that are far above anything mundane.

God bless you

Joachim Kranzen